I, Too, Can Be

SPECIAL!

To Northern Taekwon-Do Academy family, Keep reaching for your Dreams!

Your champ Darryl

Written by

Darius S. Andaya

Illustrated by

Darryl P. Andaya

Copyright © 2020 DS Andaya Enterprises Ltd.

ISBN: 9781716858505

Email: dsataekwondo@gmail.com

Website: dsataekwondo.com

All rights reserved.

No part of this publication may be reproduced in any print or digital format without the permission of the publisher.

DEDICATION

To the love of my life,
Rowena
My inspiration, my strength.

To my kids
Dana, Darson, Darryl, Darren
My hopes and dreams fulfilled.

To Everyone with Down Syndrome
And those Living with Special
Challenges

You were born to stand out,
Don't be afraid to
stand up and be recognized.

ACKNOWLEDGEMENTS

Thank you Darryl
for giving me the inspiration
to write this book.

I wish you a fruitful life
filled with wonderful
experiences and exciting
adventures.

Your mom and I
are both very proud
to be your parents and
we wish you a very happy life.

May God bless you
and keep you always.

Darryl is an English name **meaning** "darling, beloved or dearly loved". It is derived from the Old English word 'deorling'.

PREFACE

This poem is about the life adventures of, Darryl, who was born with Down Syndrome. As common to his condition, his tongue has low muscle tone which makes it difficult for him to speak. The poem is told on his point of view so that through me, he could finally tell us all the things he has been longing to communicate to the world since the day he was born.

- THE AUTHOR -

"Do you love him, this child...
    sleeping by your side

Or would you give him up
    and cast him aside?"

"What kind of
    question is that?!"
    my mom gasped,
    surprised and befuddled

As she cradled her dear baby,
    Upon her bosom snuggled.

Sweetly, calmly as he can,
 the doctor held mom's hand

Answered mom's
 unvoiced questions,
 her admonish
 and reprimand

 DOWNS: Short for Down Syndrome. At the time, mom and dad had no idea what it was.

"Your baby has downs,
 he might not be
  what you expected

So I have to ask, will you
 make sure he's
  protected?"

Mom and Dad,
in unison and harmony

Pledged love and support
to their tiny little baby

"He is our child,
With us is his home

We love him no matter
the added chromosome."

Down Syndrome is caused by the presence of a third copy of chromosome 21.

True enough,
　I was loved, cared for,
　　all my nights and days

　while my parents and siblings,
　　adapted to my ways

　It must have been hard,
　　So incredibly challenging

　But my family
　　bonded together
　　　in ways most encouraging.

Mom worked at home
   always present when we call

While Dad did all he can
   to put food on the table

My brother and sister
   took turns
      keeping me company

I was showered
   love, joy and patience.
      I was abundantly happy!

As a baby, more or less,
I was like any other

I was cute, I was cuddly,
not too much of a bother.

I loved dancing, and singing,
and bum-scooting on the floor

With great speed and agility,
through the house I explore

Darryl favoured bum-scooting rather than crawling to move about. He does this at great speed, usually travelling with one leg bent in front, the other foot on the ground while pushing with the opposite arm.

I kept to myself,
played quietly on my own

Though I do love company,
when I'm not alone

I loved music, movies, tv,
and playing with toys

I loved banging the drums,
but not so much the noise.

As years go by,
and my baby friends mature

I stayed young at heart,
in mind, body, and demeanour

"Just can't be helped,"
some people would declare

"He is what he has,
Life is just not fair."

Yet slowly I changed,
progress was acquired

What others learned at two,
I began learning at five

I went to school, developed new friends

Had hundreds of firsts,

Even had my heart broken.

He was crushed when his "crush" refused to dance with him at his Grade 7 prom.

I started learning new skills,
Used computers and tools

Played baseball, golf, bowling,
Learned to follow the rules

I wanted to be Superman,
Be fit, valiant, and strong

Though all I really aim for
was to fit in and belong.

 Though learning is delayed, DS kids want the same things everyone wants, to be happy and fulfilled. Be patient.

I learned at my pace,
Kept a slow steady progress

Learned right from wrong, and best I can,

Do little acts of kindness.

> The key to their success is to find what they are good at and help them stick with it.

'Twas a hard feat but search I did For my little special trait

How do I fit
on this puzzling world?

What in me makes me great?

Then one time, at Ate and Kuya's class, while my father supervises

I saw their fun playing little games while throwing kicks and punches

ATE: (A-te) Filipino word for big sister
KUYA: Filipino word for big brother

A spark lit up in
my young mind,
"Well, I can do that too!"

So I jumped and imitated
All the movements that they do.

The unofficial student,
high kicks and splits
like Jacky Chan's were easy

Of course it helped
That my low muscle tone
Made me just so naturally flexy

After a while I got tougher,
swifter, and stronger

And learned to conduct myself
with high morals and honour.

Darryl won Best Talent at his Grade 12 talent show. Although he loved the trophy, He performed solely because of the love of performing.

Finally, I found my place,
A talent that makes me shine

A new skill that feels natural
One I can call mine

A talent I share
With my family and friends

I hope not to have to use it,
Taekwon-Do's
art of self-defense.

When I started Taekwon-Do

Under my Coach/Dad's guidance

**Not much was expected
No one thought I would advance**

**But I stayed,
observed, and persevered,
And always kept a high spirit**

Trained in ways that champions did,

Not a thought wasted to complain nor quit.

For years I trained and toiled
with my brothers and sister

Their progress was faster
but it was never a bother

Darryl received his blackbelt after 10 years of rigorous training mixed in with mainstream students.

I kept my eyes on the prize
Not the black belt nor the medals

But the joy of belonging,
That I too can be special.

Ten years passed,
I, at last,
earned my black belt

Competed among
world's best
won a couple metal trinkets

I loved the fame, the praises
The glorious adulation

But nothing compares
to hopes, dreams, and goals
Reaching their fruition.

Two time World champion at the 2019 International Special Needs Taekwon-Do Games in New Zealand (plus a silver, a bronze, and a trophy for 4th Best country.)

Through patience
and perseverance,
which I had in abundance

Though double the work I toil
for the same small pittance

Special needs I may have,
A disability, some would say

But I work harder than most,
Just to learn how to play

These cards I've been dealt,
my "Chromosome Twenty One"

A winner's hand for betting
men, but what really have I
won?

I may be different,
but so is everyone
So why do some think less of
me?

But I shake it off...
I'm alive,
I am loved,
I'm a trove of positive energy!

This year, I turn twenty
No longer a boy, but a "man!"

Still struggling with speech
but I trust in God's plan

As I have never ever failed
to keep on believing

On the Lord above,
On myself and my kin,
or the friends I've been keeping

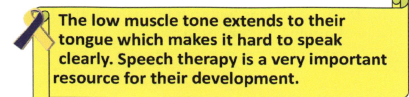

The low muscle tone extends to their tongue which makes it hard to speak clearly. Speech therapy is a very important resource for their development.

For as long as this world
I live in keeps on turning

Bringing joyful todays
and wondrous tomorrows,
a life worth living

I will continue to learn,
I will continue to reach

I will fight on, charge ahead

The SD logo, which Darryl made himself, stands for Super Darryl. This is his "achiever" mode when he wants to do something extra special. By turning DS to SD, maybe, without knowing it, this is his way of turning his condition around.

Down syndrome is characterized by physical features which makes the condition distinguishable by sight.

All along I have the answer,
it's written in my face

This is neither bad luck nor curse, but a show of God's grace

I may not know why,
I may sometimes feel doubt

But I'm not here to fit in,
I was born to stand out.

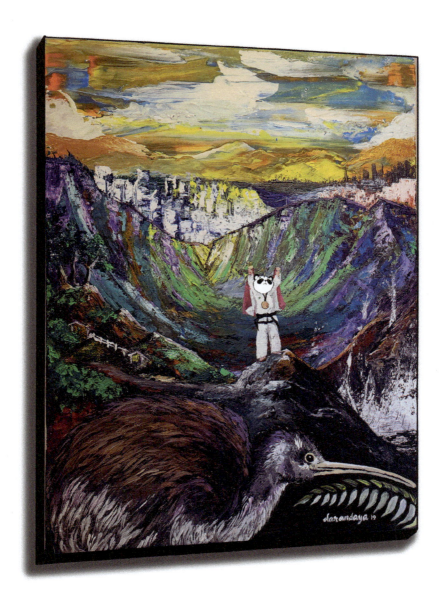

I am the boy in the mountains
with hands held high

Draped in my land's banner
with my eyes in the sky

I challenge great odds,
I do the unexpected

I lift all hopes
of all the disenchanted

The "Boy in the mountains" is an acrylic painting by the author to commemorate Darryl's win at the 2019 International Special Needs Taekwon-do Championships in New Zealand.

Though I learn not
at someone else's timetable

Given the chance,
I will always prove that I am able

To do things others,
better capable than I can

On my own special way,
I can learn like anyone

After receiving a high school diploma in 2017, Darryl continues to take classes to learn about his community and hopes to someday live independently.

To live, to dream,
to love and create

To express my desires, feelings,
to argue, debate

To say what I mean,
to show where I stand

On issues of the world, my life,
Or any matters at hand.

These are my hopes,
my roadmap to tomorrow

When I'm living my dreams,
somewhere under a rainbow

When I've learned how to live
Independent and free

When decisions for my being
is made by only me

That day will come,
the process has started

As I've begun exploring life,
Trek to regions uncharted

Slow and steady,
One step in front of the other

I will be seen and will be heard,
Like a flash of lightning
and mighty roar of thunder.

53

I will be fruitful, I will shine,
I will prove myself special

I will do what must be done,
to squeeze out my potential

**I will prove myself
to the world and you**

**That yes, just like
anybody,
I CAN BE SPECIAL TOO!**

OTHER GOOD READS FROM KINDLE

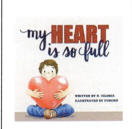	**MY HEART IS SO FULL** By Nelrose Viloria A wonderful story about a cheerful and curious young boy named Victor and the adventures of his growing family. Victor learns a valuable lesson about life and love and discovers the special bond between siblings as they welcome his baby brothers into their family.
	**SEE YAH IN THE MORNING** By Kaye Liao Banez Bedtime is often not a fun routine, but it can be--with a little imagination and reassurance that all will be good the next morning!

THANK YOU TO THE FOLLOWING GRAPHIC SOURCES

- Favpng.com
- Pngwave.com
- Dlpng.com
- Freevector.com
- Pngio.com

 Visit us at dsataekwondo.com

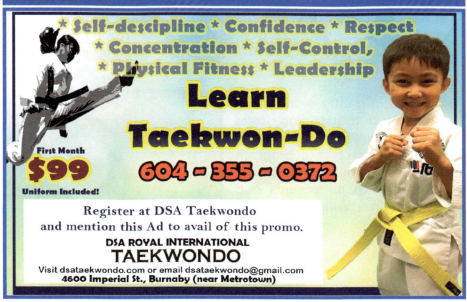

ABOUT THE ILLUSTRATOR

Darryl Andaya, started training in Taekwon-do at age 8. He was diagnosed with down syndrome at birth but that didn't stop him from achieving his goals. In 2017 Darryl, was awarded the black belt in Taekwon-Do and he has since started in assisting to teach the Little Dragons class (age 4-6 years old).

 2019 is a big year for Darryl. Aside from receiving the George Klukas Award for Outstanding Achievements from the Down Syndrome Resource Foundation, he became one of the first World Champions at the First International Special Needs Taekwon-Do Games held in New Zealand. Darryl brought home 4 medals: two gold, one silver and one bronze, as well as a 4th place Trophy for Best Country for Team Canada. This is a huge achievement for a single delegate team.

Darryl is currently working on his speech and attending classes for community inclusion and work experience in a program called Gateway to Adulthood. He lives with his parents and siblings in Vancouver, BC, Canada.

ABOUT THE AUTHOR

Darius Andaya, lives in Vancouver, BC, Canada with his wife and four kids. He is a BS Computer Science and Master in Business Administration degree holder and has been working 20 years in the dental field as an Office Manager and over 30 years as a coach and a Certified International Instructor in Taekwon-Do. A 5th degree black belt, he teaches Taekwon-Do after school hours at his own school, DSA Royal International Taekwon-Do.

A multiple-time Canadian champion and coach, DSA shared his love of the sport with all his kids, including Darryl, who was born with Down Syndrome. In 2019, he founded the Canada Special Needs Taekwon-do Association and started teaching Taekwon-do at the Down Syndrome Research Foundation. He has also championed the inclusion of a Special Needs Division at the provincial level Taekwon-do tournaments. Its aim is to provide a level playing field for competitors with Special Needs. In 2019, DSA together with his son, Darryl, won gold medal at the 1st International Special Needs Taekwon-do Games for the mixed abilities event with their exciting routine on Pre-arranged Sparring.

Mr. Andaya is an entrepreneur, a coach, pilot, painter, singer, dancer, a sport enthusiast and a devoted father and husband. He is a big advocate on inclusion and providing opportunities for people with disabilities especially in his sport of Taekwon-Do.

Contact 604-355-0372
Website: dsataekwondo.com
Search DSA Taekwondo on social media.